WELCOME TO THE WORLD OF
Porcupines

Diane Swanson

D1495892

Whitecap Books
Vancouver / Toronto

Edited by Elizabeth McLean
Cover design by Steve Penner
Interior design by Margaret Ng
Typeset by Tanya Lloyd
Photo credits: Victoria Hurst/First Light iv; Wayne Lynch 2, 4, 6, 14, 18, 24;
Thomas Kitchin/First Light 8, 10, 12, 20; Robert Lankinen/First Light 16;
Tim Christie 22; Lynn M. Stone 26

Printed and bound in Canada

Canadian Cataloguing in Publication Data

Swanson, Diane, 1944–
    Welcome to the world of porcupines

    Includes index.
    ISBN 1-55110-856-9

    1. Porcupines—Juvenile literature. I. Title.
QL737.R652S92 1999   j599.35'974   C99-910841-7

The publisher acknowledges the support of the Canada Council for the Arts
and the Cultural Services Branch of the Government of British Columbia for
our publishing program. We acknowledge the financial support of the
Government of Canada through the Book Industry Development Program
for our publishing activities.

The author gratefully acknowledges the support of the British Columbia
Arts Council.

For more information on
this series and other
Whitecap Books titles,
visit our web site at
www.whitecap.ca

Contents

World of Difference

PRICKLY PORCUPINES WEAR QUILL-FILLED COATS. No wonder they're called pricklepigs, quillpigs, and quillers. Even the word porcupine comes from French words that mean "spiny pig." But porcupines are not pigs. Like mice, squirrels, and beavers, they're rodents—animals with four front teeth built especially for gnawing.

North American porcupines are the second biggest rodents on the continent. They're at least as heavy as a pail of ice cream, but some weigh much more. Masses of long hair make them look bigger and heavier than they really are.

A porcupine's coat is usually quite black, but it might be mostly brown, gray, or cream—even golden.

1

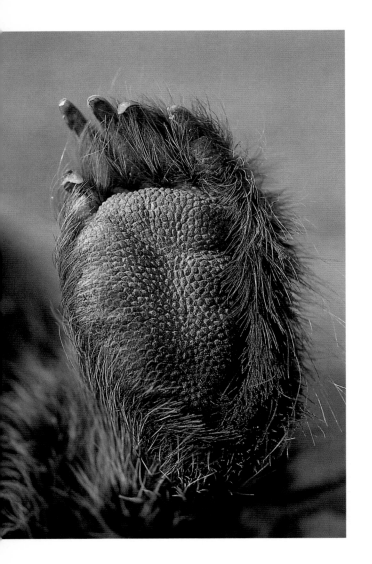

Different kinds of hair make up a porcupine's coat. Soft, fluffy hair forms a thick layer of fur all over the animal—even its underside. In cold northern winters, this fur is almost as warm as sheep's wool.

The longest hairs in the coat are called guard hairs, which help the porcupine shed rain. They look like thin quills, but the real quills are special hairs

Sharp claws and non-skid feet help porcupines climb trees.

2

with sharp, pointed ends. Most of the time, they're hidden by the guard hairs. Beneath the porcupine's tail, the quill hairs are short and stiff, like bristles on a brush.

Porcupines also have long whiskers, which help the animals feel their way at night or inside dark caves. Even in daylight, their small button eyes cannot see far. But porcupines smell well, often standing up on their back legs to sniff around. They hear well, too, especially low-pitched sounds.

QUILLPIG CLIMBING

Like every tree climber, the porcupine has special gear for the job. Long, curved claws on all four feet slip into cracks and folds along the bark. Strong muscles in its back legs grip the trunk. And the pebbly bottoms of its feet help keep them from slipping.

Climbing down—backward —the porcupine presses its clublike tail flat against the trunk. The coarse bristles on the underside prevent sliding. Even so, porcupines tumble from trees quite often.

Where in the World

Snow didn't keep this porcupine home in its den. It's hungry.

PORCUPINES HERE, PORCUPINES THERE. In North America, they find homes in many places: forests, rangelands, sea coasts, and mountains. Mostly it's food that makes their homes appealing. The more food a place offers, the more porcupines it attracts.

Nighttime is normally when porcupines explore their world and eat. During the day, they rest and sleep—often in trees—but they might snuggle into dens to escape rain, heat, or cold.

Porcupines stay active even through northern winters, but on very cold days

5

Porcupines usually sleep in different trees than the ones they feed in.

they spend more time inside their dens. They cozy down in caves, hollow trees or logs, and buildings such as barns and sheds. A few porcupines may share one den. Six of them once moved into an empty cabin, sleeping inside the ovens and chimneys.

Waddling on short legs, porcupines don't travel far in any weather. During winter, they travel even less, usually feeding in trees close to their dens. The snow doesn't bother them much. In fact, if it's firm enough to walk on, it helps them reach food.

Porcupines live on every continent except Australia and Antarctica. North American porcupines live in many areas in Canada and the United States and in part of northern Mexico. Their closest cousin is the Mexican porcupine, which lives on tall mountains in Mexico and parts of Central and South America.

WITCH TREES

Near their winter dens, porcupines often create spooky-looking "witch trees." Years of feeding on bark—mostly in the treetops—changes the way the trees grow. Their trunks become stunted, and their branches twist about in weird ways.

Witch trees make ideal dining spots for porcupines. They're easy to climb. They sprout plenty of yummy, easy-to-reach branches. And their thick tops help protect the porcupines from bitter winter winds.

World Full of Food

IT'S EASY TO GNAW WOOD, WITH PORCUPINE TEETH. The front pairs—top and bottom—are strong and sharp. A tough orange coating protects their outer surface. As the porcupine gnaws, it sharpens these teeth by wearing away the backs faster than the fronts. Because the teeth grow for its whole life, they don't ever wear out.

During the winter, porcupines use their big front teeth to scrape off bark. Then they eat the tender woody parts of shrubs and trees. They also nibble needles on evergreens.

In warmer months, porcupines snip off

Their dark orange chompers help porcupines chew through just about anything.

9

This cast-off antler,
shed by a deer,
makes a healthful,
mineral-rich meal
for a porcupine.

twigs and eat new buds and leaves. They munch on fruit, especially apples—but they usually toss away the cores. A lot of their summer food, including grass, clover, and dandelions, grows down on the ground. And some grows in water. Porcupines wade or swim in ponds to feed on salt-rich plants, such as water lilies and pondweeds.

They also nibble salty soil.

The porcupine uses a set of flatter teeth, called cheek teeth, to grind up food. A gap between these teeth and the animal's big chompers lets it tuck its lips behind its front teeth. That helps to keep bark chips—and frosty winter air—out of the porcupine's mouth.

Sitting up on its hind legs and tail, the porcupine can use its front paws and claws to hold food while it eats. It can also reach out and pull a branch close, then dine on the juicy leaves and bark.

Pass the Salt

The smell of salt attracts porcupines, often several at a time. If they find potato chips at a campsite, they dive right in. They also get salt from human sweat on axe handles, boat oars, canoe seats, steering wheels, and leather boots.

The glue in plywood is salty, so porcupines sometimes chew on wooden signs and buildings. And they feed on salt that's spread on roads to control ice. If it collects on car tires, porcupines chew those, too.

World of Words

PORCUPINES DON'T HAVE MUCH TO SAY. That's because they spend a lot of their time alone. They talk a bit when they're looking for mates and caring for their young. And sometimes they talk to warn enemies—such as fishers, mountain lions, wolves, and people—to leave them alone.

Porcupine warnings come in three forms: sight, sound, and smell. The sharp difference between the light and dark hair on an adult's back and tail makes it easy to spot at night. If an enemy appears, the porcupine turns its back and uses

Expressing interest in a mate, a porcupine may stand—even walk—on two legs.

13

Quills exposed, this porcupine is telling the photographer to back off.

its body like a flag. "Go away," it's saying.

If that doesn't work, the porcupine tries sound. It shivers all over, then lightly closes its jaws. That makes its top and bottom teeth c-l-a-t-t-e-r together. The sound is soft, but scary, lasting up to 30 seconds at a time. If necessary, the porcupine repeats it again and again.

Sometimes sight and sound warnings fail. Then the porcupine tries talking through smell—a special odor it makes only when threatened. One whiff is enough to make your eyes water and your nose stream. It comes from an organ in the skin just above the animal's tail. Even a young porcupine is able to make it.

All this talk wouldn't be any good unless the porcupine could back it up with action. If an enemy dares to ignore the warnings, it might get a snout or a paw full of sharp quills.

PORCUPINE LULLABIES

On spring and summer nights, a mother porcupine talks to her young pup. She grunts softly, coos like a bird, and clicks her teeth now and then. The pup snuggles close, drinking her milk and making high-pitched coos and grunts. Their special "lullabies" can last more than half an hour.

When the mother leaves to get her dinner, she might call to her pup, and it might whimper back. When it's older, it often makes a soft "mmmmmm" noise as it looks for its mother.

Prickly World

PORCUPINE QUILLS KEEP A PORCUPINE SAFE—most of the time. After all, it has about 30 000 of them. Except for its snout, ears, and underparts, quills grow on the porcupine's entire body. More form on the back and tail than anywhere else, but the longest ones are usually on its shoulders. Some can be longer than the blade on a table knife.

Most of the time, the quills lie flat, and they point backward. But if a porcupine feels threatened, they spring up and point out in all directions. Turning its prickly back on its enemy, the porcupine often

With thousands of sharp quills in their coats, porcupines must groom themselves carefully.

17

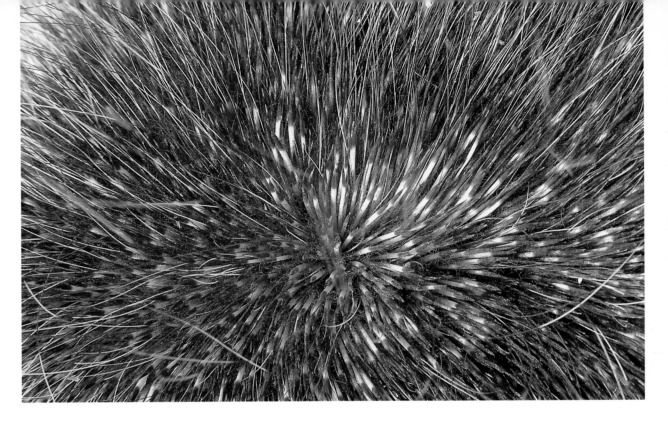

Touch these dark pointed tips even lightly and you will be stuck with porcupine quills.

presses against a rock or tree to protect its front.

If an animal tries to grab the porcupine, the quills pull out easily. They are only loosely attached. Their sharp points pierce the attacker's skin and work their way inside. Grease on some of the quills helps them move more deeply into the muscles.

Using its strong, clublike tail, a porcupine can also strike its attacker. It drives the shorter tail quills right into its enemy. No porcupine can throw its quills—as some people believe—but it strikes so fast that it looks as if it can.

Losing quills to protect itself is no problem for the porcupine. It just grows new ones. It regularly sheds and replaces quills and other kinds of hair. Sometimes it shakes itself like a dog to remove loose quills and leaves them behind in a prickly pile.

Porcupine quills can cause pain—even death by piercing such organs as the lungs and stomach. Tiny barbs cover their sharp tips, making the quills hard to remove. Once they puncture an animal's skin, the barbs expand. As the animal moves, its muscles pull the quills in deeper.

Even porcupines can suffer from the quills of unfriendly porcupines. But they're quite good at removing them. They sit up on their back legs and tail and use their front feet and teeth to yank out the quills.

New World

IT'S A GOOD THING A PORCUPINE IS BORN IN A BAG. The pup arrives fully quilled! Its mother uncovers it by licking off its jellylike sac.

A newborn porcupine pup has its eyes wide open, and it already has eight teeth. At this stage, the pup's four front teeth look more like needles than the "chisels" they will become.

At first, the pup's quills are soft. They harden about an hour after birth. The pup already knows how to use them to defend itself, but it can't whack its tail with much force and its quills are quite small.

Sticking close to its mother, this young porcupine crosses water by walking along a log.

21

Nose to nose, this mother porcupine seems to be trying to calm her frightened pup.

Most porcupines are born in April or May, but some don't arrive until late summer. In the safety of a ground-level den, a mother gives birth to just one pup in a year. It weighs about as much as two oranges.

Until it's six weeks old, a porcupine pup isn't strong enough to travel far from shelter. Its mother stays nearby and feeds the pup often with milk from her body. The pup also starts nibbling plants when it's only seven or eight days old. Lunch is usually followed by a nap.

A young pup can't climb well. When its mother heads up a tree to sleep, she leaves it hiding. It might be tucked among some rocks, beneath an old log, or inside a hollow tree. When nighttime comes, she climbs back down to check on her pup and make sure it's well fed.

NIGHT OF THE WOLF

The night was dark, but that's when the porcupine pup felt safest. Curled up at the foot of an evergreen tree, it waited for its mother. Sniff, sniff. It tried to pick up her smell. It cried a little, like a human baby.

Then there were footsteps. Something was moving softly through the woods. The pup sensed a wolf heading its way. Raising its quills, it swung around, ready to slap its tail. The wolf backed off. It may have discovered prickles before.

Small World

PORCUPINE PUPS DO MORE THAN PLAY—though they seem to play often. They "fight" with their mothers, biting them gently. And they raise their quills, whirl around, and whip their tails about. Sometimes, they even attack the wind. Play helps pups develop the skills they need to defend themselves. It helps them exercise, too.

Porcupine pups also have lessons. They learn how to groom their long, thick hair by combing themselves—front to back—with their claws. By following their mothers, they find out what foods are good to eat and

Still and safe! A porcupine learns to hide in a tree.

where to get them. And they learn how to choose safe hiding and resting spots.

As they get stronger, porcupine pups try wading in shallow water and swimming. They also practice their tree-climbing skills. A mother porcupine in a tree may call out to her pup, urging it to leave its hiding place and climb up.

A small pup holds on tight with three feet while it moves one foot up the tree.

The pup grows fast. As it gets bigger, it travels farther with its mother on nightly feedings. It starts spending some nights alone, looking for its own food, when it's about three months old. At that age, the pup's warning colors have appeared, and it can protect itself from small enemies.

One night—usually in the fall—the mother leaves her pup forever. If it's a lucky porcupine, it might live to be 10 years old. Not many porcupines in the wild live that long.

PORCUPINE PICNICS

It's a good thing that tree-climbing porcupines drop food as they feed. That makes it easier for other animals to get more to eat. When porcupines snip apples off trees, for instance, they knock some to the ground, creating a picnic for chipmunks.

Porcupines nip off tree branches to gobble up the leaves, nuts, or juicy wood. When these branches drop down, rabbits and deer feed on them. A picnic like this is especially welcome when snow buries their usual food.

Index